The Service Call Blueprint

Field Tested Strategies for Higher Revenue

Second Edition

by Roger Daviston

Table of Contents

Foreword... 1

Measure Where You Are 2

The Path That Brought Me Here.. 6

Anchors 9

The Service Call Blueprint Steps

Pre Arrival 10

Arrival 14

    Slow Down.. 19

Diagnose.. 21

Presentation 24

      Patterns.. 32

      Menus 34

      Payment and Billing... 38

Execution 40

    Execute the Work Now... 40

Wrap Up... 41

    Anchor the Call 41

    Service Agreements 43

Leadership.. 44

Purpose 46

Personal Growth is a Process... 49

Shiny Objects 50

Script Templates

Service Agreement Greeting & Presentation of Concerns 53

Demand Service Call Greeting and Presentation of Repairs 55

Water Heater Presentation Script 56

FOREWORD

Roger Daviston was a client in the early 1990's. Current wisdom at that time was that contractors always lost money in the first quarter. (Maintenance agreements were not as prevalent in the early 1990's). I helped Roger price his replacements to make a profit. Once he had this last tool, Roger broke that conventional wisdom. He made a profit in January, February, and March.

Was Roger the only contractor who could do this? I wasn't sure. So, I had Roger present his strategies for generating revenue and profit in the slowest times of the year to the contractors I was working with at the time. They implemented his processes, and they too earned a profit in the traditionally slowest part of the year. And, they increased their profits year-round. Roger's methods worked.

You can be profitable year-round too! This white paper shows you how. Implement these strategies, processes, and procedures to be in the black year-round.

If you are sick of having to dig out the rest of the year because of a poor first quarter, then change what you are doing because it isn't working. The answer to what does work is on the next pages.

Fair warning. These strategies are easy to implement. They are also easy NOT to implement.

The choice is yours.

Ruth King
Profitability Master and nationally recognized
consultant to the HVAC industry

Measure Where You Are

Hello everyone. My name is Roger Daviston and welcome to the Service Call Blueprint. I'm really excited that you have decided to take the time to read this book. My hope is that you will learn something extremely valuable and apply these principles to create a better outcome for yourself.

Why did I write this book? I wrote this book to show you how to get more money from each service call. If you implement the strategies in this book you can achieve significantly better results.

What is your average ticket now? Think about it and go measure it. Here's what you need to do. Take all your service tickets and add up the total revenue and divide that answer by the number of service tickets that have money on them. That will give you an average number. The average number that I see for heating and air conditioning companies is less than $200.00. Plumbing is higher.

Please don't read any further until you answer the question, "What is my average service ticket?" Go do it now. Measure a year's worth of data. Stop now and go do it. It's a major problem in this industry that people watch, listen and learn but never take action. Take this important step before you go any further in the book.

If you have any questions about how to do this, send me a quick email at roger@rogerdaviston.com. I am always happy to help.

If you take these principles that you're about to learn and implement them in your business, you should expect to see an increase in your average service ticket of 100% to even 200%. Legally I cannot guarantee any sort of increase whatsoever, but if you take action it is my experience that these are the sorts of results that I have witnessed time and time again.

Now, take the answer that you arrived at two paragraphs above (what is my average ticket) and double it. Then multiply that number by the total number of calls for the year that you measured. The results should be staggering.

Let's look at the math while making a few of the following assumptions:

1. Assume that we have 4 technicians and they run on average 15 money calls per week and we have 48 weeks per year. This takes into consideration holidays, sick days and vacation days.

2. Assume that our average ticket is below average at $180.00 company wide.
3. Assume that each technician ran 720 money call (15 tickets x 48 weeks = 720)
4. Assume that the company ran a total of 2,880 service calls. (720 tickets per tech x 4 techs = 2,880)
5. Assume that we collected $518,400. ($180 average ticket x 2,880 tickets)

Look what happens to total revenue as we increase the average ticket:

Current revenue $180 x 2,880 = $518,400
50% increase $270 x 2,880 = $777,600
100% increase $360 x 2,880 = $1,036,800

These numbers are not bull. I know what some of you are thinking because I have been there. This is not a blue sky promise. Take a look at the following results from a client of mine. He would be happy to talk to you and verify that the information is true if you have any doubts.

Study the chart below. This is why you must implement the Service Call Blueprint. This is a before and after comparison of 611 calls (six weeks before and six weeks after).

We compared the average ticket amount before and after. If you'll notice we generated $42,684.00 more in revenue as a result of coaching the process change. Also, notice that Tech 6 decreased.

Table 1

	Before	After	Change	Number of calls	Change in revenue
Tech 1	$301.00	$438.00	$137.00	105	$14,385.00
Tech 2	$456.00	$621.00	$165.00	78	$12,870.00
Tech 3	$314.00	$397.00	$83.00	106	$8,798.00
Tech 4	$372.00	$468.00	$96.00	60	$5,760.00
Tech 5	$199.00	$225.00	$26.00	123	$3,198.00
Tech 6	$309.00	$292.00	-$17.00	139	-$2,363.00
Total				611	$42,648.00

3

There is a reason for this. He did not do what we asked him to do and the boss allowed him not to do so. Notice also that Tech 6 ran more calls than anyone else because he rushed. Tech 6 is costing this company $10,286 in lost revenue. This is assuming that we replace him with a person who achieves an average of the top three techs. If we replace tech 6 with a winner we make even more.

This is a leadership issue. We know that Tech 6 does not do what we ask of him because we listen in to the virtual ride alongs and the boss only yacks. Recently, the boss agreed with me and we are limiting Tech 6 to only 3 calls per day. The boss also told him that he must comply and the boss is now listening in to every presentation and meet and greet on our VRA online platform.

I implore you to measure your numbers before you go any further in this book. What gets measured and focused on will improve if you have the leadership skills to get your people to do the things that make them successful. I can help you with that too, but that's another book for another time.

So, the Service Call Blueprint works if you do what it asks you to do. After all, I wrote this book so that you can get more revenue per ticket and make a net profit of 15% to 20%.

So what was my big Aha Moment? When I owned my heating and air business, I used to sell complete systems and I learned that if I gave people options they would generally pick something in the middle. But sometimes they shocked me and picked the most expensive. My big aha moment happened one day when I showed a customer four options to replace his system and he picked an option that I thought was worth more than his house and I went, "WOW!"

If I had not followed the process that Tom McCart taught me, which was to show all of the options possible, the customer would have never picked it. So, I learned about how people buy. People buy based on menus. People don't buy based on what we think they should buy, they make their own choices. For example, we don't go into McDonald's and listen to them tell us what we want. We look at all the options on the menu and make a choice.

We could go into McDonald's and satisfy our hunger for much less than their average ticket. If McDonald's took down their menu, I submit to you that their average ticket would plummet. Offering this same type of choice in the service business is something we must learn how to do.

Don't let yourself be confused. There is a difference between the terms "flat rate" and "menus." Flat rate is not a menu. A menu is derived from your flat rate book after bundling together a repair along with upgrades, cleaning and other restoration services that would be beyond the scope of what is needed to only repair what's broken.

Flat rate is derived from estimating how much time it's going to take me to change out a specific part if I already know which part it is. I also know how much I must charge per hour and how much I must mark up the part. Therefore, I can derive a flat fee for the work that I propose. The menu takes it further and we will study that further in later sections of this book.

The Path That Brought Me Here

Before I go any further, I want to answer the question, "Who is Roger Daviston?" Allow me to give you a little history about the path that brought me to this place in time.

I graduated from the University of Alabama with a B.S. in corporate finance and investment management in 1982. I finished college in three years after taking a year off after high school. I washed dishes at The Claim Jumper restaurant in Park City Utah and skied most days in the winter. I took classes every summer to catch up and finish college on time.

The stock and bond market intrigued me. I really enjoyed the money and banking classes and was fascinated by how the banking system and the Federal Reserve operated. So, I got a job as a government securities trader at a bank in Birmingham, Alabama.

This bank was a primary dealer for FNMA, Federal Home Loan Bank and the Farm Credit Bank. I traded these agency securities, treasury bills, notes and bonds, mortgage backed securities (like GNMAs), bankers' acceptances and commercial paper.

It was a very interesting job. I traded bonds for two years and was promoted to be an officer of the bank at twenty-four years of age. I actually hated this job even though I was successful at it and had been given a 25% raise after the first year. I was not a great fit for the job and I did not like the confinement of sitting in front of four television screens, talking on the phone and fighting with sales people all day long. I was not quick on my feet with the math but I did learn a lot. It was a great place for me to grow personally.

I sat in a room with about fifty sales people who worked a telephone all day. Their customers were other banks who purchased and sold their bonds to or from us. These sales people were high performing earners and some of them made more money than the bank president. All the sales people were paid about twenty-five thousand dollars per year salary but the rest was commission. These commissions were paid each quarter.

So, my first experience in the business world was in an environment of "sell something, make something." And, a lot of money they did make. I watched a young man make thirty thousand dollars in one week because he had a great relationship with a banker and it paid off for him at the right time.

I was exposed to high performing individuals who were successful if you measured success by income. I saw what sales was all about and I watched the successful salespeople. Just by watching I developed a good psychology about what it would take to be successful at sales.

I resigned from my position at the bank and started Daviston Insulation of Atlanta Inc. in 1984 with my father. My father financed most of this business but I did contribute about $5,000 to the equity. I was 24 years old.

I took what I learned about sales at the bank and applied it to the new construction insulation business in Atlanta, Georgia from 1984 until 1988. We sold that business to a national competitor that required me to stay with the new company for a set period of time.

I got restless not working for myself as I had grown up in an entrepreneurial family. So I began to look around and ended up purchasing a really tiny heating and air conditioning business in Bessemer, Alabama, a suburb of Birmingham, where I was from. If you do some research on Bessemer, it is listed as number five on the FBI top 100 list for violent crime. It was a place that was declining, yet in 1989 I purchased a business there. It was my hometown and I looked forward to building my first business that I owned by myself.

Hamrick Heating and Air had been around since nineteen thirty-eight. It was originally called Barney Gray Tin Shop. I had a phone number that had been in the white pages for a very long time. I had an answering machine, one install crew and Mr. Hamrick ran service calls.

The first day at Hamrick Heating and Air was June 1, 1989. We signed the papers the day before at a law office in Bessemer. I'll never forget that my first experience was getting in a Toyota diesel mini pickup truck in the passenger side. Mr. Hamrick, who was seventy-five years old, was driving.

If you can picture this, I was sitting with my knees up close to my chin because of the returnable coke bottles that were on the floorboard. To make it worse, this truck was painted a loud blue color with the words "Alabama Heat Pump Dealer" written everywhere. Don't misunderstand me. I love Alabama Power and they helped me in my business. The problem had to do with the choice of text and color.

So off we went to fix an air conditioner and take a snake out of a package unit. In Alabama, we used commercial package units to heat and cool houses that had low crawl spaces.

That's how I got started in the heating and air conditioning business. I did not know anything about heating and air. I didn't even know that I must be a certified contractor by the state of Alabama to be in business. The state marshal found out and came by. They gave me grace, allowed me to study, take the test and did not run me out of business. That was a blessing and I want to thank them for that.

Let's fast-forward eleven years. I sold Hamrick Heating and Air Conditioning in the consolidator wave in the late nineties. Hamrick Heating and Air had forty employees, twelve telemarketers with a manager, seven install crews, four salespeople and other office folks. We made double-digit net profits on sales of about 2.8 million, even in the first quarter of the year in mild Alabama winters.

I only had two technicians because our market was such that people didn't have the money to repair things, but they could finance a new system. We were extremely proactive. I required all the sales people to generate their own leads by cold calling or canvassing neighborhoods. I learned this at the bank, so my psychology about how to conduct business was very different from the industry's. Our business model was not as seasonal because we were proactive. This is why we were profitable each and every month.

We built a sales culture. We focused on finding someone to talk to who needed or wanted what we had. We produced a 9% net profit in Alabama during the first quarter of 1999 while paying myself a six figure salary.

I want to give you the same amazing results and teach you how to do this with your service techs. It's a simple process.

I started the Daviston Group in 2001 after selling Hamrick Heating and Air. The reason I started consulting was because I really enjoyed helping people grow and become more in my own business. This is what gave me great pleasure and joy. This is what I want to do for you.

Anchors

So, let's get started on the service call process by talking about what anchors are and why are they important. Anchors are similar to Pavlov's dog experiments. Pavlov rang a bell and fed the dogs. The dogs salivated when the dogs saw the food. After a few pairings of this sequence of events, ring the bell feed the dog, ring the bell feed the dog, the dogs salivated without seeing the food. The bell alone elicited the salivating state.

Another way to say this is that the bell became an anchor to elicit salivation in the dogs. Fire off the bell, fire off the state. The bell controlled the dogs. Anchors are stimuli that call forth certain emotional states in us as humans.

For instance, can you hear the sound of your mother's voice calling out to you when you were a small child? Probably so, right? If you notice, you are probably feeling some sort of emotional reaction to this sound. I don't know what it is. It could be a good feeling or a bad feeling. The point here is that the sound of your mother's voice elicits the emotional state and is the anchor for the response of how you feel. You had no control over the emotion. It was just fired off much like lighting fireworks.

Anchors have been established in your customers and we want to avoid the ones that fire off negative emotional states. Also, while we are there we want to establish and even activate some resourceful anchors, and it's easy to do. We do this because we want the customer to be in a good emotional state when we drive away. I'll show you how to do that later.

Let's look at the steps in The Service Call Blueprint. Each step has certain things that I want you to do.

1. Pre-Arrival
2. Arrival
3. Diagnostic
4. Presentation
5. Execution
6. Wrap Up

Pre Arrival

Study the history file and become very familiar with all of the past invoices and what was done before you drive up. It's also helpful to know any past estimates in addition to service work. We want to know what kind of relationship we have with this person. Is this person a prospect, customer or client? The difference between these three is the level of trust that has been established.

Let's explore the difference between these three levels of business relationships.

Who is a prospect? This would be the person who has never given us any money. We need to know how they found out about us and why they called us. If they were referred to us there is a higher level of trust. If they found us online there would be a lower level of trust. Prospects who don't know us should be treated differently because they don't know anything about our process or procedures and are new.

How I connect with a prospect would be very different from how I would connect with a long-time client. I would show gratitude in a different manner. I might say, "I understand that you found us online. Thanks for deciding to call us. I know there are lots of other companies to choose from. My goal today is that when we leave you're very satisfied with the experience. Knowing that there are many choices online, what made you pick us?"

I would like to get them talking. When they're talking and I'm listening, they are liking me. I don't want you taking thirty minutes at the door, but I do want you to have a short conversation where you are mostly listening.

I'm going to want to know who has been servicing their system and fixing it when it breaks. This is a good question because it can expose their pain. You can see the pain on their face when they answer, "nobody, we've never had it serviced." People know that neglected mechanical things are going to break more often.

I also ask that question to explore the possibility that they are unhappy with their current service company and, if so, why or what happened. You can find out very important issues that may need to be addressed by learning the history of the relationship with the past company. We want to avoid making the same mistakes the other company made.

And that leads me to another question. If it's a new prospect and this is our first trip to their home, how do we know the history? We ask them just like the doctor. I took Inna, my wife, to the doctor recently. I go with her because I am the Russian English translator. This was our first trip and the nurse drilled us on her past history. It took ten minutes. When the doctor came in, she also drilled us on the past history by asking the same questions while reading what the nurse had typed in the computer system.

Prospects give us a tremendous opportunity to grow our business. The lifetime value of a good client over the fifteen years could be tens of thousands of dollars. You are the hands and feet of our business. The prospect sees and hears you, and how you execute this part of relationship building could prove to be very valuable over the life of this potential client.

Don't blow it. Slow down and focus on them because we want to move this person to the next level of the relationship, which is called customer.

Who is a customer? A customer is a person who has given us money in the past for our services. There is some trust and confidence in our ability. A good illustration that compares prospect to customer would be dating. A customer is someone who we have been out with a few times. These few dates were pleasant, we had a good time and there seems to be potential but there are still a few questions in our mind. We have not spent enough time with them to develop a totally trusting relationship.

What is a client relationship? Trust is the difference between the customer and client relationship. All of us have client relationships and customer relationships. When you reach the level of trusted advisor, you then have a client relationship. I have many client relationships where I am the trusted advisor. The relationship and best interest of my client is ALWAYS ahead of the money because the money will flow from the relationship in time.

I have a great client who asked me to coach and train his customer service representatives. My thought was that we should not spend any resources on coaching or training before we diagnose the potential return on investment. He agreed, so we hired a friend of mine who lives in Ukraine to listen to calls and measure the conversion rate.

We determined a low potential for growth because the conversion rate was already extremely high. Most of the calls were from clients. Remember, they trust us and just want us to come out. We lost a few prospects but not many. We could have improved and gotten better, but to spend money on this at that time would have been the wrong choice.

My client thanked me and he used his resources in a more productive way. This cost me revenue today but not tomorrow.

Don't miss what I just said. I see service companies put extreme pressure on technicians to perform and bring in revenue on every call. I once watched an electrician cheat a customer. I became aware of it after we left by asking questions. I asked the technician why he did that and he said that working at this company put extreme pressure on him to bring in money.

Wow, we talked about his shame and guilt. We talked about doing the right thing and that he did have other choices. After more talks and ride alongs, he decided to leave because the constant pressure to violate his own values repulsed him. Eventually, he left the service industry and he is doing very well.

Knowing the history tells you what level of relationship you have with the person and it also communicates competence and confidence. It implies that you care about them and are there for them. Can you imagine the doctor not asking you about your past medical history?

Don't make the mistake that Levi made. Levi is a technician client of mine who I have coached and trained for three years, and he really got into trouble one day with a good client. You never want to get into trouble with anyone, but especially not with a great client.

Levi and I headed out to his first call and he did not check the history file even though he has been taught how important this is. It's one of those things that is easy to do but easier not to do.

The only information Levi knew was to do an air conditioner planned service. I was with him and he knocked on the door and the call went downhill from there. The client was an elderly widow who was a bit nervous and Levi made it worse. She was nervous for a very good reason, but Levi had no knowledge as to why and he got blindsided. It all could have been avoided if we had the knowledge. Levi looked incompetent, not confident and he was not a good representation of our company because he was lazy in executing process. The process includes checking the history before you arrive.

At the door Levi introduced himself.

Mrs. Jones, in a nervous voice: Are you Mike?

Levi completely ignored her question and began to tell her why he was there. But she would have nothing to do with Levi's agenda.

"Are you Mike?" she screamed out.

Levi answered in a sort of southern tone: "No ma'am, I'm Levi."

"Well, where is Mike?" Mrs. Jones screamed with a frustrated, angry tone. "They promised to send Mike."

Levi explained that sometimes the schedule changes and that he was sent to do her maintenance and not to worry. He could do everything that was needed. Oh boy! That was the wrong thing to say as I listened to the next question out of Mrs. Jones' mouth.

"Oh, good then you know about my unit??????" she asked in a polite, more relaxed tone.

Levi is now in really big trouble because he does not know about her unit. He knows nothing about her, her unit or what happened in the past. Mrs. Jones had a right to be upset and frustrated with us and we appeared incompetent simply due to laziness and lack of execution.

We called the office and determined that last spring Mike replaced Mrs. Jones' air handler in warranty because its evaporator coil was leaking. Mrs. Jones had purchased a new system from us and it quickly had a warranty issue. She was nervous about this system. Mike had assured her that everything would be okay and that he would return. We arrived with no knowledge of the past and that really upset her. It would upset me too.

There are many reasons to check the history. I have often found that by reading the history file, I'll say too myself, "Wow, we really need to bring this up." Maybe other past estimates that were waiting to be sold because we elicited some things when we started the conversation with the customer.

It's easy to check the history file, so please check it. I know you can run call after call with no problems but you never know. I promise that you're missing opportunities and you may not even know when the customer picks up on your lack of interest in them.

Arrival

Exit from your truck immediately and do not linger in the driveway. So on the pre arrival you must take care of all necessary paperwork and other things before you arrive. This will free you up to get out quickly. Do not pull into the driveway and sit in the truck and do anything. The customer has been waiting. Be respectful and move with urgency.

This is the negative anchor that I want you to avoid. Probably in the past some other service person from another industry sat in the driveway and then the customer felt frustration. It made the customer feel bad. So now when you do the same thing it triggered that emotion. We don't want to trigger any negative emotions before we greet the customer. It's a wise thing to be ready to exit your truck upon arrival because you could fire off the anchor like a firecracker.

Check your appearance before you arrive. What the customer sees could hook a very bad emotion in them also. This is a place where we want to install an anchor. We want to install a positive emotion. If you look clean, professional and sharp, this implies and installs in them that our work is clean, sharp and professional. If you look sloppy, dirty, sweaty and possibly even smell bad, the call will start off badly. A service call that starts well is much more likely to end well.

I can still today feel the negative emotion when I think back to a plumber that arrived at my house over seventeen years ago.

I called a plumber to come out to my house because we had problem with water leaking into the floor from under the shower. He arrived a little late, but that was not the main issue. He knocked on the door, I let him in and he said, "Hey, sorry I'm late. I just ate lunch."

Well, I already knew that he had eaten lunch because I could see it on his shirt. Can you picture this? I could see the fresh ketchup stain on his shirt. What a terrible state his unclean appearance put me in. I could even smell that restaurant on his clothing and I new where he had eaten. It was a BBQ place that I loved, but I did not want to be smelling this in my kitchen.

I now have two negative experiences in the first five seconds. I have a really bad visual and olfactory experience that put me in a negative state. I could even smell onions on this guy's breath. He has elicited from me a very bad emotional state, not by his words but by his looks and smells. He engaged my since of smell and vision in a terrible way and was not even aware of it.

I completely shut down and my brain closed. I couldn't even listen to anything that he said. I just led him politely back to the master bath, not listening to anything he said. All thoughts were about how soon I was going to get this guy out of my house, all because he had ketchup on his shirt and he smelled like onions.

Check your appearance. Those of you who are smoking in the truck or taking a smoke break before you arrive, you are not helping yourselves. If you're serious about your average ticket you will stop this behavior. I do not like to smell smoke and many others feel the same.

Call the customer before you leave for the home. However, I don't want you diagnosing the problem over the phone. I just want you to reach out by phone and start the connection process. I want you to say something like this:

"Hi Mrs. Smith. This is Roger with ABC Heating and Cooling. You're my next appointment and I am on my way. The GPS says 20 minutes and if I have a problem I'll let you know. Is there anywhere in particular that you want me to park?"

That's all I want you to do. Do not diagnose or get into anything having to do with their pain, problem or system. It is not the time to do this. We will do this at the correct time but there are other things that we must establish first.

I only want you to connect briefly with the customer. It gives you a sense about their emotional state like are they mad, upset, or calm. Do they sound glad to hear from you? I want you to give them a heads up about where you are because it will help them relax and not worry. Then, when you pull up and get out of your truck looking and smelling great, you'll be ahead of the call. Remember, a service call that starts well has a better chance of ending well.

Get out of your truck immediately without tools. I want you to listen to the customer and have a conversation with the customer. We don't want to start working yet. You may take a nut driver in your back pocket, out of sight, but I don't want you to get started diagnosing yet.

We must establish control in the beginning. The first three minutes of the service call is where you establish control of the process. The customer controls the content but we are the boss of the process. I'll say this again. A service call that starts well has a better chance of ending well.

If you knock on the door with your heavy tool bag, this implies you're ready to work and the customer will have a tendency to rush you towards the equipment. We will look at the equipment, but now is not the time. If you knock on the door with empty hands it interrupts their pattern and forces them to use their brain and talk to you, especially if you start asking the right questions.

I coached a technician who would pull up in the driveway, exit his truck and walk to the door of his van. As I watched him, it was as if he was getting ready for battle. That's what it looked like to me. He would put on his knee pads and put his dust mask around his neck. His seventy-five pound tool bag was in hand and his refrigerant gauges were draped over his head and on his shoulder like a shield for battle. He was literally scaring his customers to death.

When he changed his behavior and arrived at the door empty handed, started asking questions and listening to the customer, he had much better results. He increased his replacement appointment setting rate for the comfort advisor and the replacement sales from his new behavior increased by $250,000 in a short six months. This was not the only thing we changed, but it was one of the factors in his success.

Ask or wait for permission to go into their home, don't barge in. Permission is usually given visually so don't ask for permission if they gave it with a nod of the head or by standing back to let you walk in. Once, I was invited in to teach a company whose employees had been taught to ALWAYS ask for permission. These guys were like robots. The customer would invite them in with a nod and then they would ask for permission. Have you ever slow danced and you felt out of sync with your partner? That's what it was like. It was an uncomfortable rapport breaker.

Human interaction is complex. Be natural, open and honest in your relations with everyone. There are some good skills and best practices, but the best practice is to be yourself and be natural.

Control the service call by asking questions, not answering them. If you are answering questions, educating the customer and trying to woo them with your product knowledge, they are in control. You never know what unnecessary subject you might talk about that might hook their anxiety, fear or send them online to educate themselves and compare.

The way that you establish control is to quickly introduce yourself and then quickly ask them how you can help them today. If you already know them, use your common sense and be natural in how you greet them. You could say, "Hi John, it's good to see you, what brings us out here today?" If you have no tools, it implies "let's talk."

I know that you already know why you are there because it's on your dispatch. However, the process of communication does not give justice to the speed of thought. This is not a book on communication but let's look at something important here.

The entire idea of what the customer wants to communicate to your dispatcher is in the customer's mind's eye. The customer has to use words in an attempt to convey the totality of all his thoughts. When the customer does this, he goes through a process of generalization, distortion and deletion to convey his thoughts. We all do this.

Think about what I just said, "We all do this". This means the dispatcher does the same thing to you. He deletes, distorts and generalizes what he was told. Now, as a technician you are two steps removed from the customers' reality and the customers' reality is really not reality so you are three steps removed from it. If your company has a CSR department and dispatch never talked to the customer, you're four steps removed from reality. This is why gossip is so destructive. By the time the rumor spreads, it's often not even close to reality.

I want you to hear the customers' best description of their reality. So ask them when you greet them, even if you think you already know. I listen to thousands of greets and I've never heard a person complain about asking them, "Why am I here?" or "What brings us out here?" Have you ever shown up to fix a sink and the customer told the office it was a problem with the toilet? I would imagine you could think of an example.

I can think of one ride along where dispatch told us that the customer wanted an estimate on a new faucet. However, when I asked what brings us out here today, I heard much more detail, pain indicators and opportunity that was not on the dispatch. We sold a very nice $1,000 service call based on what I heard from the mouth of the customer by asking that question.

Relax and listen after you ask that question. We want to hear about the customer's pain and frustration. You can't do this by showing up dressed for battle like the example I gave you earlier, with your head down and your mouth and ears closed. You must ask and then you must listen. As you listen you must ask other questions that reverse this process of deletion, distortion and generalization.

When you ask questions and listen in this manner, you gain understanding of what their agenda and expectations are. Customers feel affirmed when we understand them, and when a customer feels affirmed he feels connected to you. Feeling connected is the essence of rapport. You establish and gain rapport by asking and then listening at the door, hallway or wherever he takes you. Just listen.

You now have the affirmed customer and a better understanding of the situation. Now we must share our agenda with them. I am assuming this is a demand service call, which means they called us because something is not working and the office advised them of a service call fee. Matt Koop, the developer of "The New Flat Rate," teaches a simple script that I agree with that simply confirms this with them by saying something as simple as the following:

"I just want to clarify with you that the office did share with you the service call fee of $79.00." If they did not understand, explain it again and get agreement.

We have another agenda too and I need to get their agreement on it. I want to show them a menu of options after I determine what needs to be done, and I want to gain permission to do this. I want to pre-frame the process by leading them in that direction before I get there. This is called future pacing and establishes more control.

Here's what it sounds like to me using some of Matt's words and mine also.

"Mr. Jones, I'm going to go back to my truck and get my tools and get started. I don't know how long it will take me to determine the fault. However, once I do, I would like to show you all your options for taking care of it today. If you choose one of those options today, I will be able to waive the service charge fee for you. How does that sound?"

Now the customer has a clear expectation of your process and has agreed to it. Many folks don't realize that we can fix their problem today because many service companies don't fix problems the same day. I would submit to you that excellent customer service is solving the customer's problem today.

Slow Down

This is a good place to stop and speak directly to the owners of the business. Many of you rush your technicians and I know why. Your technicians don't have the communication skills to make money on each call, so you think the solution is more call volume. I understand your psychology. However, you must change your psychology to profits and revenue per call from call volume. Think more money with less call volume. Is the goal of the business net profits or call volume?

The following story will illustrate my point. John and I went on his first call of the day, which was a service agreement fulfillment for one customer at their own home and then around the block at their rental home. The owner sent John a text message around 10:30 AM and said "Hey, get out of there, you've been there too long." The owner's psychology is hurry.

I called the owner and told him, "Do not disturb John, we have a big fish in the water, we can see him. He looks hungry and we think he might consider our solution."

We presented five options from five hundred dollars to twenty-four hundred dollars and the customer picked the most expensive solution. The technician handbook said we should be there about six hours and we had to go to the supply house to get what we needed because none of these parts were on the truck. We called dispatch and gave them a heads up that we were booked the rest of the day. It was now dispatch's problem to juggle its schedule.

John sold his day by 10:30AM. The revenue for the day was $2,400 and the call volume was one call. You must develop a new way of thinking about the service all process from call volume to revenue volume, and to do this you must limit the number of calls. It is impossible to increase revenue per call without decreasing call volume. You will increase billable hours with less calls.

The oil business is in a period of identity crisis, and I believe it's because the size of the market shrinks each year. I have heard the sentiment, "service is a necessary evil" that comes from the industry. I get it. You have oil and oil is very profitable. I would submit that the oil model is more profitable than the service model. And I also agree that with the oil model you increase your profits with volume of accounts. I understand why you believe in volume of calls. More profits are derived from more deliveries.

Oil is a commodity and service is not, but it can become a commodity if you allow it to. High value service is a different model. Think fewer calls per tech and more net profit per tech. Slow down and establish this first and then grow call volume by training and hiring new people.

In the above example, we only did one call and sold $2,400. Most of you are racing through five calls and have an average ticket of less than $150. To learn a process, slow down and require technicians to execute the process. You can easily double your tickets, but in doing so you shrink your call volume. It's mathematically impossible to increase your billable hours per call and run the same amount of calls unless you overwork your technicians, and that leads to burnout and high turnover.

Clarity is power. If you identify with the belief that "service is a necessary evil" this book is a waste of your time. If you identify with it then be that person. Give the tune and vacs priority and get them done on time. Give excellent customer service and deliver the oil in a timely manner. There is nothing better than knowing who you are and living it. And you will make money. Be excellent at who and what you are and be clear about it.

However, it's very difficult to sit on two chairs. How do we get all the tune and vacs done and increase your service revenue? The answer is not an easy one and outside of the scope of this book. However, I do know that when you book a technician's day in advance and he sees his schedule, he will rush himself. And you can't blame him because he wants to get home at a reasonable hour. To ask him to take the time to look and present is possible, and yes, you can schedule the work for later, but in reality, the tech rushes himself because it's 3PM and he's got two more calls. I know this because I have been in the truck with them and we have talked about this very subject.

Diagnose

Now, let's move on and look at the diagnostic step. Resist educating the customer and "no ball bearings" (I'll explain this shortly) during this time. Go to your truck, get your tools and then start your process. How you diagnose is up to you. This is your skill, not mine. Sometime the customer follows you around and this is okay. But resist telling him what you are finding, even if they ask, because it's not time to tell them yet. We tell them in the presentation step, and you only tell them that which they need to know.

If you start sharing with them what you think or what you have found, they start asking questions and you lose control. You also risk telling them something that may scare them and put them in a negative state. You could trigger one of those anchors that we learned about earlier in the book. It isn't that we want to hide anything from them, it simply isn't the right time to present your findings.

I'm sure that you are wondering what I mean by the phrase, "no ball bearings." David Sandler, who built the Sandler Sales institute, which is now a worldwide sales training company, told me a story about a husband and wife who were shopping for a china cabinet for their dining room.

As the story goes the husband says to the wife, "Honey, I love it."

Wife: Me too.

Husband: It will fit perfectly against the wall.

Wife: Yes, and the lights are beautiful. I really love this one.

The salesman jumps in and adds, "Yes, and look at the drawers. See how they slide so nice and smooth? They're made with ball bearings."

The wife says to the salesman with a look of panic on her face, "My two-year-old choked and died on ball bearings".

Well, so much for that sale and way too much information. I learned another lesson form David Sandler: sell today and educate tomorrow. There was no need for her to know that the drawer was made with ball bearings. Ball bearings are everywhere. The words "ball bearings" was an anchor that triggered a real bad memory. You never know what you might say that could hurt you. Ask questions instead of educating. The amount of information you gain is directly proportional to the amount of your ticket. The more information you give, the lower your ticket. Develop the habit of asking, not telling.

The salesman only needed to ask if they wanted the china cabinet, but he couldn't resist educating them. In other words, simply ask a question like, "What would you like to do?" Resist sharing what you are learning about and what you are finding during the diagnostic step. It could hurt you if you tell it to them at that time. Remember, the amount of our ticket is directly related to the amount of information that you receive, not give. How do you receive information? You receive it by asking great questions.

Another issue with telling is that you also risk the customer going over to his computer, Googling what you told him and looking up how much the part costs. This formulates a budget in his mind that is not realistic and causes you to have sales resistance when you present solutions. In this case, you have allowed the service process to be commoditized.

Take your time and do not rush through the diagnosis. You build value in your service when you take your time and don't rush. Explore the entire system and search for other issues, much like a doctor examines you when you're sick. The doctor checks much more than what you are complaining about. We have a tremendous risk of liability if we miss something and an accident occurs. If you know it's a simple issue that you have seen hundreds of times and you go straight to it and it takes a few minutes, that's fine. But don't stop there. Go over everything. We charge a diagnostic or service fee, so give them great value in return. Take twenty or thirty minutes minimum and do a great job.

Matt Koop with The New Flat Rate teaches a simple way to think during the diagnostic process. Look for reliability issues. Don't fix anything, but look at wires and see if there could be some potential issues that could come up later. Look everything over, and if you see anything else, make a mental note and don't talk about it. We will build a menu of options later.

Look for performance issues during the diagnosis. Make a mental note of anything you see that is causing this system to work at less than its original performance, or maybe something that you could add to enhance the system's performance. This could be cleaning and restoring the system to like new condition.

Look for safety issues. Pay attention. Take your time. Is there anything that you see that could be unsafe? This could be electrical, fuel delivery or venting concerns. You are the technician. Slow down and look. How many call backs could we prevent by going through this methodical process?

Are there any health issues? This could be related to safety concerns or air quality. Standard throwaway filters don't filter much. There are many opportunities to bring up health and air quality issues.

Presentation

When you start your presentation, move away from the source of the problem. Do not show your solution to the customer while standing over the problem. Don't ever show the solution to replacing a condenser fan motor while standing over the condenser. I saw a plumber put his price book down on the toilet while he attempted to present a toilet repair. It's terrible. You may ask, why is it terrible?

Well, let's go back to our anchor lesson. The toilet that is broken is potentially an anchor that triggers the emotion of frustration or something else negative. So, when they are standing close to the toilet they may feel frustrated. I simply want you to move them away from the broken piece of equipment because it interrupts the pattern of the emotion that's in the moment.

They will have a different sensory experience when you move them. They will see and hear something different, which changes their state. I don't really care where you take them. I would make it a comfortable place where we could all sit down to talk about and look at the options.

Let me illustrate this for you. I was with a salesperson and we met with a lady who was referred to us by another client. So, this lady was a prospect but we had established a certain amount of trust. Her friend referred us and we were standing on her friend's good favor.

My client, the salesperson, began telling her all that was wrong with her furnace and air conditioner while she was standing there looking at it. This was the first mistake. Remember, "no ball bearings." This is the diagnostic step, but it's a sales call. It's not time to talk. This is the time ask and listen.

It gets worse. He told her about another problem that she had with her water heater and this triggered panic because her mother ALMOST died from the same problem. Mr. Salesperson now tried to rescue her from her panic by giving her solutions as we all stood there and looked at the source of her panic, the water heater. This was another big mistake.

Our prospect was so engulfed with panic that nothing the salesman said connected with her. She did not receive anything he said. I stepped in and asked if we could walk outside for minute. It was a spring day in New Jersey after a long winter. The sun was warm. The sky was blue and the birds were chirping. Simply moving from the dark musty basement and interrupting our sensory experience made us all feel better.

She relaxed and we began to talk about a future room addition. We suggested that it would make sense to come back later and meet with her and her husband. The lesson here is to simply move away from the source of the problem before you give solutions. A presentation has a proper place and time and it's not during the diagnosis step and it's not in front of the problem. Many of us have a difficult time waiting because we can't wait to help the customer. Be patient. We will give them solutions at the proper time and place.

What's the bottom line? Moving the prospect to another physical location changes their sensory experience. This change in sensory experience simply changes their emotional state from feeling bad to feeling better. The better feeling opens them up to hearing and receiving your message. It's a simple thing to do, but easy not to do.

Present five or six options for every repair. You may be thinking that this is impossible to do, and you may be correct if you don't change your own thinking. Your psychology about service must shift to be able to do this.

Let me give you an example. Alabama Power invited me to give them an estimate to replace a split system heat pump that conditioned a guardhouse at a steam plant. This thing was engineered to withstand an earthquake. It was a lesson for me about possibilities. Yes, the split system was overkill and not needed, but the word here is "need." Many times we buy things that are not needed, but we want them. A hard start kit is not needed, but someone may want one. A new contactor may not be needed, but people do buy them to increase reliability.

I am asking you to think past need and open up what is possible with an unlimited budget. Think about possibilities for excellence in service that would cost five or six times the basic needed repair to get the system running. It is not your responsibility as a technician to decide for the customer what to do. Put the weight of responsibility where it belongs and that is on the customer.

Option One: First, present what is broken only. Unbundle the other things that you may do. Just present the minimum, least expensive, and fastest solution. Boom, you're done. This first solution should have no extras and should come with a very short warranty. We had a tail light warranty on all "gas and goes" (added Freon) which lasted as long as you could see us drive off. We did nothing extra to prevent another breakdown. Option One is to replace what was broken and get it running. This is the bare minimum repair only.

Option Two requires answering a question that you ask yourself. What could I do to take twenty minutes and add this additional service time to look for anything that could cause another breakdown that would be unrelated? Look deeper and pay closer attention to loose wires or anything that grabs your attention. Add this twenty minutes to the price. If you find something simple, fix it too. This could be replacing terminal connections if they look bad. Use your own wisdom and knowledge to answer this question. If you are already doing this, unbundle it from your first repair and then bundle it back in as your Option Two. Go a step or two further and see what you can do to prevent something from happening and charge for that service over and above the minimum.

Option Three requires answering another question. Are there any enhancements that I could add to the system to make it better than it was when I arrived? As an example, let's pretend that a customer has a bad capacitor in a condenser. You could enhance that system by installing a hard start kit, new contractor or both. If you think further you could even add an option for a solid state contactor. Simply think about how you could make this system better than it was when you arrived.

Think about a stopped up condensate drain line. How many times have we cleared the drain? Could it be totally rebuilt and restored? How many times have you gone back to that same drain system as a call back and never given the customer the option of making the drain system like new? I love to watch the show *Fixer Upper* on HGTV. Think total restoration. It will help you build the menu.

Simply think in your mind from the least expensive solution to overkill and three options in between. Inna and I lived on the upper east side of Manhattan in one of the most expensive zip codes in America. I promise you that we were one of the poorest people in the neighborhood.

Living there changed my thinking about possibilities. One morning I was walking to the bank and noticed a store that might have a nice headset for my computer. I was met by a clerk who quickly asked me what I was looking for. I told him. He smiled and said, "Our clients are the ultra rich. We provide them with sound system solutions that are out of this world. Our least expensive solution is $15,000. We are having a champagne reception in about an hour to show them some of our newest sound systems. I don't think we have what you are looking for."

This company culture had clarity. They clearly knew their identity and were not afraid to express it to me. He was not rude but he was assertive. He never made excuses for the expense of their systems. So why do we? Don't be ashamed to show your best and most expensive and outrageous solution. Ask bigger.

Our industry tends to be like the Dollar Tree stores. Dollar Tree, Inc. is a public company of retail stores. They sell a variety of things and everything in the store is less than a dollar. It's interesting to look around and you do find some great buys. However, everything in there is cheap, there is a lot of junk and that's the market segment Dollar Tree targets. We can target everyone simply by showing all the possibilities.

Option Four could be adding cleaning that would bring the system to like new condition. Think about detailing a car. You can get an automatic car wash anywhere from five dollars to over 30 dollars. In addition to that, you can get a detail cleaning that is several hundred dollars. A clean system works better and lasts longer. Start offering different levels of cleaning for your fourth option.

Matt Koop recommends adding another level of service, like a one-year inspection a year later. This inspection would be for the purpose of checking the work that was done today, and because of that higher level of service, you could give a better warranty.

Yesterday, my car started making a noise and it sounds like the power steering assist is going bad. Inna, my wife, reminded me that we had this same noise fixed about a year ago. We paid about 500 dollars to get this fixed, but now I'm not sure if it's the same issue. However, I probably would have spent more money if I were offered an inspection of the work a year later in exchange for a better warranty. Ask bigger and more often. "Ask, seek, knock and you will find" is a favorite scripture of mine.

Now, let's look at a menu that I hand written while running a service call with a technician in New York State.

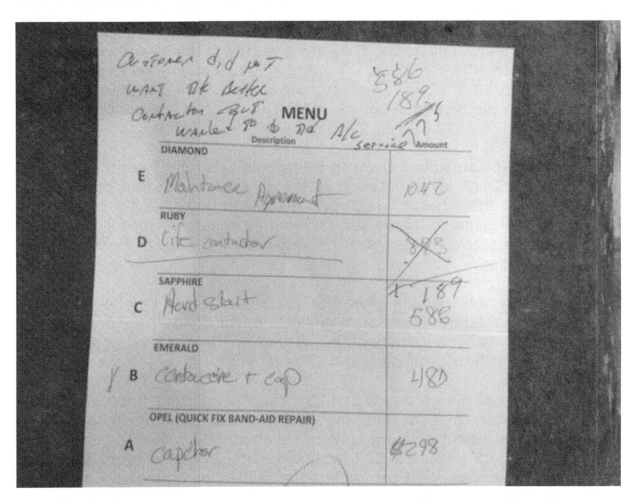

This is a menu that the technician hand wrote as I walked him through answering the questions that I gave you earlier. This customer had a bad capacitor. The customer was not home and I ran the call for the technician. He did the work as I was teaching him this process.

The children were home and this new customer had found us online. I asked the son to call his dad and I did my meet and greet with the father over the telephone. Here's what it sounded like.

Roger: "Hi Mr. Jones, this is Roger with ABC Heating and Air. Thanks for calling us out today. We appreciate it. How can I help you today?

Mr. Jones: "Hey yea, thanks for coming out. I'm not sure what's wrong. I'm an electrician and I don't have enough room in my panel for my generator in the winter. So, each winter I disconnect my condensing unit and use that spot for my generator. When I reconnected the condenser the other day, it wouldn't run. It's sixteen years old. So I have no air and that's why I called you out."

Roger: "I understand, and I heard you say that it is sixteen years old. Who has been servicing it for the past sixteen years?"

Mr. Jones (with pain in his voice): "Nobody. It's never been serviced."

Roger: "Okay, I got it. So just to confirm: Did the office share with you the diagnostic fee of $78?"

Mr. Jones: "Yes they did."

Roger: "Okay great. Let me share with you what I would like to do and then you tell me if it's okay. We will get our tools and diagnose the issue. I'll call you back and show you a broad range of solutions and you can tell me which one fits your budget. You're the boss. How does that sound?"

Mr. Jones: "It sounds great."

Roger: "Okay, just one more question. How were you planning on paying us today and not being here?"

Mr. Jones: "That's no problem. I left a signed check with my son."

Roger: "Okay, we'll get started and call you back and go over your choices."

So, we got our tools, walked around to the side yard and found a very old condenser, but it wasn't in bad shape. The run time in New York up in the Hudson Valley is very few hours per year, nothing like the many hours in Alabama or Texas.

We quickly discovered a bad capacitor and completed our diagnosis. So we completed steps one and two. The meet and greet was step one and the diagnosis was step two. Step three is to go back to the truck and build a menu by asking myself all those questions that I explained earlier.

Please refer to the diagram and the questions below.

1. What is broken and what is the bare minimum needed? Obvious answer: capacitor. ($298)
2. What could we do to prevent call back and other breakdowns? Not so obvious and could be debated, but we chose a contactor. Add in the contactor and the total now is ($487).

3. How could we enhance the system and make it better than it was when new? Hard start kit, which increases the total to ($586). Also, we could install an expensive solid state contactor, which would bring the total to ($873).
4. Are there any other reliability issues that we could address? Again this is debatable but he is a candidate for cleaning and a service agreement. This increased the total to ($1,042)

So, we now have a complete menu to show the customer, but in this case we are going to call him. To the best of my memory here's what the conversation sounded like:

Roger: Mr. Jones, is this a good time to tell you what we found and what your options are?

Mr. Jones: Yes. Please.

Roger: We found that your system has a bad capacitor and to replace that is $298. There are some other things that you may want to consider. Could I share this with you?

Mr. Jones: Yes, please.

Roger: Thanks. To increase the reliability, you may want to also consider replacing that contactor. If so that would increase the total to $487.00. In addition, you may want to consider enhancing the performance and make it better than it was when it was manufactured by adding a hard start kit. That would bring your total up to $586. Further, for even better reliability you may want to consider upgrading the contactor to a solid state contactor. That would increase the total to $873. In addition, you may want to invest in a yearly service agreement and, if so, that would bring the total to $1,042. So, you're the boss. What would you like to do?

Mr. Jones: Well, I know I have to do the capacitor. I get the contactor and I also get the hard start kit. I don't like the idea of the solid state contactor and I don't want a service agreement.

Roger: Okay. So, capacitor, contractor hard start kit for $586?

Mr. Jones: Yes.

Roger: Sounds good, but I have one more question before we get started. Would you like for us to clean that outdoor condenser? It's sixteen years old and has never been touched.

Mr. Jones: How much?

Roger: Let me see. (I had to calculate this because this was not on our menu but I was flexible and saw an opportunity) It would bring your total up to ($775).

Mr. Jones: Okay, let's do that too.

Roger: Great. We'll get started and call you back when we are done.

We completed all of the work and during the process of cleaning and servicing the air conditioner, we found that the indoor evaporator coil in the attic's air hander was very dirty. This is a very important point and reinforces why you must slow down.

Do a thorough check after the system is running. We cleaned the condenser and checked the operation with the gauges and noticed that maybe we had some other issues, and we did. We discovered on further inspection, because of what the gauges were telling us, that maybe we had an air flow issue, and we did.

We found that the indoor evaporator coil needed cleaning. What a surprise right? After all, this system was neglected for sixteen years. Now we have another opportunity to serve the customer even better. So, I made the call.

Here's what it sounded like:

Roger: Mr. Jones, we got the system running and it's cooling fine. We did discover another issue that you may want to address but it's up to you. The indoor section up in the attic has a coil that you may want to clean. Would you like for me to text you a picture of that?

Mr. Jones: No, just clean it.

Roger: Okay, but before we do that let me tell you how much it will be.

Mr. Jones: Okay, fine.

Roger: You total for today would be $975.

Mr. Jones: Sounds good, let's do it.

Patterns

The habits that you go through and the habits you form lead you down a path of success or failure. I can look at someone and determine his or her habits. I walk down the street and see a weight lifter, a runner or a swimmer. They all look a little different but I can tell what their ritual is.

I can look at a service technician's average service ticket and discern his rituals, too. The habits and rituals that you perform over and over will lead you to success or failure. There are rituals and habits that lead to higher average tickets and customer satisfaction, and there are rituals that lead to much lower average tickets and customer complaints.

What are your rituals and habits with the customer? Do you have a sequence of events and a standard process? Or do you just wing it? Nick Saban, the head coach of the University of Alabama, is the best college football coach in America. He gives the same answer each time they do the live interview before the kickoff. It goes something like this after the analyst gives his spin on what needs to be done.

Mr. Saban: All of that really doesn't matter. We know what we need to do to be successful and we must go out there and execute what we know to do. We have practiced and are prepared and now we need to go execute. It's really that simple. It's a simple strategy of plan and execute.

A football team is much more complex than a service call, but the best team in America has a plan and the coach expects execution. I would submit to you that if your average service ticket is dismal it's either because you have no process or the process is not executed. The truth is that there are many plans that will work. Coach Saban has a different philosophy than other coaches. What Coach Saban is good at is establishing the boundaries and he expects his players to execute. To be frank, most of the leaders in this industry don't expect their people to execute. They hope and even beg but never expect.

The difference between companies that are successful and those that are not is the leadership. The plan could be the problem. However, the bigger challenge is getting your technicians to do what is necessary to be successful. This is a leadership issue, and quite honestly, I see this as the real issue.

I spoke with a client two days ago who has this problem. He told me that they had tried a very popular system a few years ago but he could not get the technicians to "work the plan." Well, neither can he get his technicians to

32

work this other system that he is implementing. I told him that the issue was not his techs, it was him. It's what makes Nick Saban a great coach. He does not put up with players who walk outside of the boundaries he establishes, nor does he let them play if they don't execute.

Menus

Our world is full of menus and we make buying decisions based on them. The retail model always makes us look at and pick from a menu. Below is a menu from an automotive repair shop close to my home when I lived in the Hudson Valley in the State of New York. I only wanted my oil changed, but as you can see, they made me choose the kind of oil to use. I had an option from $35.99 to $76.99. I'm sure that you have seen these kinds of menus all around.

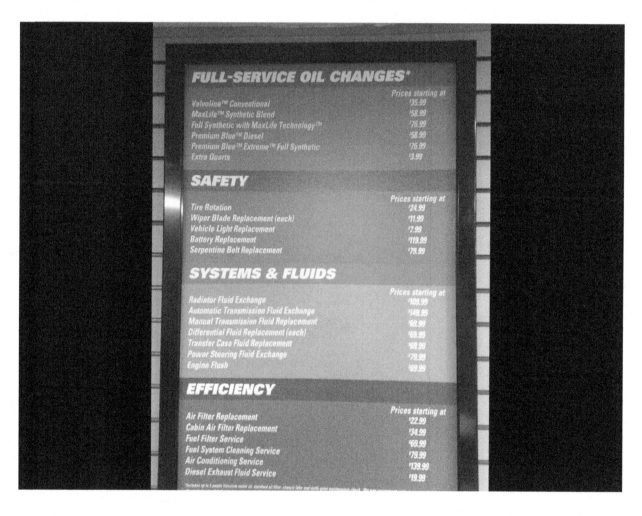

Let's look at a car wash that I will never use again.

This is a menu. Look closely. What does the menu say about their quality of workmanship? Do you notice the duct tape, the general condition of the menu? I must decide between 12 bucks and 16 bucks, but do you feel good when you look at this menu? I don't.

The menu that I showed in the service call example was handwritten and the customer did not see it because I called him over the phone. You can handwrite menus, but I believe that if you use an iPad to present menus, this does two very good things. It adds credibility to the pricing model and it adds professionalism to your process. This car wash example does neither.

I never went to this car wash again. Their professionalism not only was indicated by their lack of pride in their presentation, it carried forward in the quality of my car wash. I actually had to get a rag and finish cleaning some areas that they missed that were obvious.

This brings us back to anchors. After I paid I felt bad. Therefore, I won't pay again. If I feel good after I pay I will be more inclined to pay again. It's all about anchoring the experience with positive emotions and not negative ones. I'll talk more on this later.

Let's look at another menu at Bobby's Bike Shop in Chicago.

I ride an expensive carbon fiber bicycle that I have about $3,000 invested in. I get it serviced twice a year because I ride so much. I want the gears to shift reliably when I ride, so I get new cables yearly. If you'll notice, I have some choices to make. They allow me to choose what I want. I'll probably get the level 4 service, and while it's by far the best option for me, it may not be for you.

The point of the menu is that if you want your bike serviced you can spend from $40 to $230. If your heat does not work due to a dirty pilot light, we could clean it for $298 or replace it for $395. Or we could clean your entire furnace blower wheel, burners, heat exchanger and make it like new for about $600. We could also come later and inspect the work we did today, give you a much better warranty and charge $800 for that. What would you like to do, Mr. Customer? It's your choice.

I get push back from technicians all the time. They whine and cry and tell me customers just want it fixed and always want to know "what I would do." I always explain it like McDonald's. Can you imagine going into McDonald's and ordering just "something to eat?" You will go hungry. They're going to point to the menu and ask you to pick from it. We would do well to learn from the successful retailers in our neighborhoods and start thinking differently about the service business.

I've taken pictures of menus where Inna gets her nails done. She always spends more than the minimum on her nails. I don't know why and it's not important. The bottom line is that she does. Without the choice, she wouldn't.

How much does a heavy winter coat cost? Well, that's an interesting question. Wal-Mart coats, Canada Goose coats or Moncler coats? You could spend $200 to $2,800 or more on a winter coat. Why are we afraid to show customers our options? I think it's our philosophy and psychology. We must think differently.

Payment and Billing

You can collect payment before you do the work and after the customer makes his choice. Simply ask bigger. The scriptures say to ask and you will receive, knock and the door will be opened and seek and you will find. Let's assume, for example, that a customer has just picked an option. Here's what it sounds like to ask, according to my friend Matt Koop, who wrote a beautiful script for this purpose. All you have to do is require your technicians to ask this question.

Roger: Mr. Jones, is it okay if we go ahead and take care of paperwork now? We take cash, check or credit card.

They all say "okay" and reach for their wallet. I know what you are thinking. Fear has overtaken you and your brain is screaming that we can't do that, and the customer is going to get angry if you make him pay upfront. **We are not making him do anything.** We are simply asking. We have the right to ask and he has the right to say "no" to our request. Don't fight the customer if they say "no." This is not a policy change. It's simply asking bigger, and most people agree.

Let me speak to the oil businesses because you bill every customer for everything. You must change this for many on the service side. Customers question themselves when they are forced to look at and pay for something 30 days after the good feeling left. Buyer's remorse kicks in. The memory of the conversation gets deluded and you WILL get many phone calls blaming your technician for any number of things that were not true. You'll write a lot of credits just to keep the oil account and service will continue to be the "necessary evil."

Remember, high value service is not a commodity like oil. It's a feel-good experience that must be collected at the time of the feel-good emotion. Otherwise, you'll get a whole lot of calls and buyer's remorse. I had this happen with an oil tech who was a good communicator. He learned how to offer the option for oil additive on tune and vac and he sold a good many of them. However, we got call backs. Customers said, "Well, I really didn't want that." We fixed it by collecting at the time of the sale even though they had an open account with oil. You can separate the two.

I have helped many third and fourth generation businesses make this transition from billable service to COD. It takes a mindset shift and then you can ask for payment for your services up front. I am not suggesting this for oil deliveries. Oil is a different business from service and if you want to be successful at service you must make the shift to COD or you will just cause yourself more frustration.

I have noticed a pattern in the oil business. This pattern is an eagerness to give credits to keep the oil flowing. I have also noticed this with AT&T. They are eager to give me credits to keep my account. I believe that you have anchored this behavior much like Pavlov's dogs. Ring the bell hooks "salivate." Open the oil bill, see something extra, hooks "call and get a credit." Interrupt this pattern by collecting at the time of the extra sale.

Execute the Work Now

Execute the work that you sold right away. Do it today even if you must travel to get a part or have a runner bring it to you. High value service is not defined by rescheduling and coming back another day for any reason other than parts need to be ordered. Do as much as you can today. This also is a mindset shift that must take place. I touched on this to some extent when I encouraged you to slow down. Give your technician one call at a time and expect that he will sell his day on the first call.

Technicians should be shielded from and not stress over the schedule. A dispatcher's job is putting the right person on the right call at the right time. Dispatchers have become virtual schedulers with no verbal interaction. Their goal has become to schedule ALL calls and clear the board without respect to profits. Technology has taken the relationship and interaction away and technicians can see their entire day. This philosophy does not consider profits but only considers efficiency and clearing of the board. The more calls the technician sees, the faster he works and the less he sells.

How are we going to increase revenue per call when techs are rushed? A technician for a large oil company told me that he did not have time to present to a certain client. We had an opportunity to show a client 5 options for thermostats because his was broken. It was too much trouble and took too much time to make a $1,200 sale.

The technician who runs through three demand calls by noon on a consistent basis is wasting opportunities. If he continues to do this, send him home after three calls. It's like a baseball batter that strikes out all the time. We can't afford to give him more at bats until he improves, because he is wasting our opportunities.

Anchor the Call

Can you fix a cuckoo clock too? What a strange question to ask, but by now you should be familiar with the term "anchor." We want to install a few anchors before we leave. Another way to state this is that we simply want the customer to feel really good about the money they just spent. We do this by executing the work and charging enough money so that we can take our time and add value.

Look around and see if there is anything extra that we can do for the client that would make him feel an intense feeling of satisfaction. We want to hear the customer say something like, "Wow, I really appreciate that." We want to instill "wow."

Let me illustrate this principle two different ways. Jason, a technician, and I sold a customer a $1,400 repair on a condensing unit. We were there about three hours, but Jason tends to hurry because that's how he was trained. He was trained to rush to the next call. We don't need to rush because we just sold the rest of our day. We called dispatch and she knows that we are tied up for another three hours. We can slow down and do a great job.

I noticed three small issues unrelated to the repair that we sold while walking back and forth from the basement to the condenser outside. The cost was a few dollars in material and maybe ten minute's time. We did three additional repairs for the gentleman. The key was walking him through the house and showing him all that we had done, including the primary repairs we promised. He was excited when we showed him the three additional repairs. He even said, "Wow, guys, I really appreciate that. I did notice those things but had forgotten about them." Do you think this customer was happy to pay us for our service? Absolutely he was.

Now back to the cuckoo clock. We finished up a service call one day after having done a great job. The customer seemed satisfied but we didn't do anything extra because there just wasn't anything that we could find. However, for some reason out of nowhere we struck up a conversation about the customer's cuckoo clock. He told us that it was not working and that he had tried to fix it without success. The technician said, "Do you have the instructions? Let me take a look and see what I can do."

I sat in amazement as the technician spent about five minutes reading through the instruction sheet and then fixed the cuckoo clock. The customer said, "WOW, thank you so much." That "wow" was worth the extra 5 minutes.

Coach Paul "Bear" Bryant, the winningest college football coach in America, broadcasted each Sunday afternoon the highlights from Saturday's game. Any time a player from either team would make a solid tackle he would shout out, "BINGO." So, whenever you here the customer say, "WOW" You can say to yourself, "BINGO." That's what you were looking for. The more "Bingos" you can get in a day the better.

This principle (anchor the call) was taught in a large company and the owner understood it. This is a very successful company that has over 200 employees now with revenues of over $26,000,000 in heating, air and plumbing. So, in this culture these things were encouraged. We even saw a technician repair a lawn mower one spring afternoon. It was a nice bookend to complete the call.

Wrap up the call by anchoring the call. You do this by going beyond their expectations, making them aware of what you did, which triggers "feel good." This is the same as Pavlov's experiment. If we ring a bell and feed the dog, the dog salivates. The bell triggers "salivate." In our example, the extra work triggers "feel good." When you leave they feel good, but only if you do the next step and don't undo everything. Don't blow it.

This leads me to my real big pet peeve. Please leave the customer's house as soon as you get back in your truck. If not, this could trigger a negative emotion in the customer. The customer could have felt great after we fixed the cuckoo clock, but if we linger in the driveway, call the office, fill out paper work, look up the next call and so on, we risk him looking outside and wondering what the heck we are doing! This really bothers people and leaves them with the proverbial bad taste in their mouth. This could undo all that you did perfectly during the service call and you may not even be aware of it.

Service Agreements

Please allow me to back up. Let's do one more thing before we get in the truck and leave. Ask for permission to present a service agreement 100% of the time if the customer is a service agreement prospect. A service agreement prospect is any person who has not purchased one. Ask for permission to present. Do not bulldoze into a presentation. If and when they give you permission, simply present the benefits of investing in a service agreement and how much it is. It's that simple.

Here's what it would sound like:

Roger: Mr. Jones, can I ask you one more question before I leave?

Mr. Jones: Sure.

Roger: I see that you don't do regular preventative maintenance, and as a technician I feel that it's important in order to maintain efficiency, mechanical reliability and safety. May I have your permission to take about 60 seconds to show you how our maintenance plan works?

Mr. Jones: Yes

It's realistic to assume that an average communicator can achieve a conversion rate of about 30%. I have seen great communicators who sold 60% of their presentations. Those technicians who sold less than 30% are not asking. The reason they don't ask is likely because there is no accountability system in place. This is leadership's responsibility to establish.

Leadership

The USPS must have good boundaries. Every time that I purchase something at the post office they ask me two questions. The first question is, "Would you like cash back?" and the second question is, "Would you like stamps with that?" I have purchased stamps when I had not planned to simply because they asked me that question. I get the same questions in Chicago as I do in New York.

The USPS creates a consistent experience from my perspective because there is process in place that ensures the behavior happens. There is also an expectation that the behavior happens. Leaders and managers are responsible for making all this happen. I don't see consistency in processes and I believe that we have a leadership crisis in the HVAC industry.

I know that this generalization is broad and that there are some good leaders. However, my biggest frustration in developing human potential is lack of leadership. Companies have wasted resources and time expecting me to help them when, in many cases, as long as I'm there, things work. When I leave they don't. This problem sits squarely on the shoulders of leadership and management.

Why do some people get results and others don't? The truth is that CEOs, owners, and managers are always seeking out that next shiny object that will solve their problems and propel them from where they are to where they want to be.

The right plan is important but it doesn't guarantee success. In fact, there are probably five or six right plans for any given situation. There are lots of ways to get there and each plan has its strengths and weaknesses. No plan is perfect.

The reason I am exposing this problem is because I want to show you how to solve it. I know this problem well because I coach businesses that use the same plan, but get different results. They spend lots of money, time, and training and I watch in frustration as these good systems are discarded and even blamed.

One owner will say, "Ah, we tried that and it just didn't work for us." Another will say, "Wow, what a difference that system is making for us. I don't know how we survived without it." How could it be a magic pill for one and trash for another? It's the same system.

The answer is not a simple one. The maxim, "There's more than one way to skin a cat" is true. And the way that you decide to skin the cat will get you to the same result, a skinned cat. But getting your team to follow the "cat skinning" process is more challenging than the process itself.

Therein lies the problem as well as the answer to the question, "Why do some people get results and others don't?" How do you get your people to do what it takes to skin the cat? That is where the difference is. It always goes back to the people. Where you win or lose is with your people, not the next shiny object.

This subject will be the focus of my next book. I have written many articles about it and you can find them on my blog at rogerdaviston.com. But I digress.

Purpose

I have a deep passion to do what I do. I believe that every person has much more potential than they achieve. I believe that every person can grow and become more than who they are. Jim Rohn said, "How much should an oak tree grow? Well, as much as it can."

I think that individuals should strive to become all that God intended for them to become. And really, this is my mission in life, to encourage you to become all that God intended you to become. That starts with knowing what your purpose is. Many of us have no idea what we were born for and just aimlessly get up and go to work to pay the bills.

Allow me to introduce you to Rita because I want you to know more about why I do what I do. Rita came to work for us at Hamrick Heating and Air to be finance coordinator. I did not hire Rita. Jean, our operations and service manager, hired her.

Rita was hired to be a loan processor. The salesman would make a sale and then Rita would take the file and process all the paperwork for the loan. Everything we sold was financed either by Alabama Power, TVA (Tennessee Valley Authority), Alabama Gas or FHA Title One. There were lots of forms. TVA required seven forms, deeds to search and verify and it became a full-time job with three sales people and six install crews.

So, we hired Rita for $12,500 per year to get all this paperwork done. Rita saw what we were doing and learned our business model. Rita was a single mom who supported two teenagers and lived in Midfield, Alabama, which was a declining area. Rita had worked for a doctor prior to working for us. She was the nurse who got your chart and took you to your room. She never made much money but she had a desire to become more.

I'll never forget the day Rita came into my office and told me that she wanted to learn how to sell. I said, "Rita, that's good but we hired you to be finance coordinator and you don't know anything about sales. I would suggest that you go read this book." Honestly, not many people took the initiative to read a book that I recommended.

Reading is the main path to personal growth. So, Rita agreed, left my office and I thought to myself that that would be the end of that. Much to my surprise, Rita was back in my office a week later telling me she read that book. So I asked her what she learned. I discerned that she had in fact read this book as I listened to her explain to me what she learned. Assertively, she asked me again, "May I have an opportunity to sell?" I said, "Yes, but you must go listen to these tapes next."

Rita listened to those tapes and we had many other conversations and she began to grow personally. Rita leaned how to make cold calls, canvas neighborhoods and we gave her a few leads on Saturdays. Something amazing happened. Rita made some sales.

We paid 10% commission if you sold the HVAC system at list price. Our average sale back in 1995 was around $7,500. All of our sales people made only commission and were treated as sub-contractors. We paid Rita about $250 per week as loan processor. The average commission on a sale was $750. Rita made a sale or two and this changed her world.

Rita would make a sale and get a check for an extra $750. That was a big deal to her. We gradually moved Rita into full time sales and her first 1099 was for $75,000.

This changed my life as I watched her change hers. This is what I want to do for you, your technicians, sales people or anyone else in your business. I simply enjoy the joy that I get by watching people grow into their human potential.

When I experienced the joy of helping Rita, it changed me. I wanted to do it again. Rita propelled me on a five-year journey questioning why I was born. I sold my business because of this journey. I do this for the joy I experience when someone has the courage to change.

Rita gave herself a 600% raise because she became a sponge and read everything that she could get her hands on. She went to a Tom Hopkins seminar and flew to Arizona on her own dime. She grasped how to make a cold call and generated many of her own leads, much like the insurance industry expects. She took a Dale Carnegie course at night and invested in herself.

The HVAC industry is seasonal business but it doesn't have to be. Rita was like me in that she believed if she knocked on doors and made cold calls that she could set appointments and sell systems. One day she picked up the white pages, started dialing, set an appointment and made a sale during Christmas week when the weather was mild. Who among you has the desire and commitment to do that?

I heard this just yesterday. "Roger, I don't know what to do. We just don't have any work and the phones aren't ringing." Sound familiar? The answer is to find a person who has desire, a good outlook, doesn't make excuses and is willing to do what it takes to be successful. And if you look in the mirror and don't see that person, it won't ever translate down into your culture.

Most of you have hired people who think like you do. They believe that you owe them leads and that they deserve leads. And you believe it, too. Dr. Michael Semon taught me that fairness is a deception. We don't owe and we don't deserve. Another truth is that if you sow in tears you'll reap in joy. It's okay to cry while you knock or dial that phone. Just don't sit around and wait on it to ring. Go ring it.

Personal Growth is a Process

People grow and change at their own pace. Everybody changes over time. Some change faster than others and every person can change. This change and growth happens by repetition, reinforced with coaching and accountability. This process can happen in groups, one on one, online, in person or a combination of the two.

Change does not happen at a seminar any more than spiritual growth occurs by going to church. Church is full of dead Christians who come and listen every Sunday but never implement the spiritual disciplines that they are learning. Learning and doing are two different things. To do so takes accountability, mentors and commitment to yourself and another person who you can trust. I have three very wise gentlemen that I reach out to often for support and correction.

Money is the result of the relationship and people must have good relationships with their clients and coworkers. Good relationships facilitate unity, and the success of the business is a function of unity of purpose or clarity. The scripture says that unity commands the blessing. Without unity, you are not going to have success. Healthy relational skills build unity.

Chris Bishop is a client of mine in Rocky Mount, Virginia. I have worked with his team for three years at the time of this writing. His business grew 55% in the first two years that we worked together. This is what he wrote a few months ago:

"Roger, I was thinking this morning about my growth, the company's growth, and how the employees had grown. It dawned on me that we started doing this in March of 2014. In just 2 years we grew the company 55%. But what means the most to me is to see the growth of the people. I thank you for challenging me, and helping me grow knowing that the company can only be as big as the leader. My reward is seeing how everyone has improved his or her lives at work and at home. Again, I just want to say thank you from the bottom of my heart for what you have helped us accomplish."

It struck me that Chris experienced the same thing that I experienced when Rita grew. Notice that Chris' reward was "seeing how everyone has improved their lives at work and home."

Shiny Objects

The Service Call Blueprint is a shiny object, and the truth is, it's not the only one that will work. If you want to make improvements in your business, you must become a great leader.

Leaders are planners, delegators, coordinators and motivators. Leaders focus on the personal development and growth of their people and understand human potential. Rita had potential and I helped her tap into it by encouraging her to read, study and grow. She changed her own life by becoming more and tapping into her potential.

You have tremendous human potential too, just like Rita and Chris Bishop and his employees. I studied just about everything Jim Rohn published. I never met him in person but wish that I did. He said that a person does not get paid by the hour but gets paid for the value that they bring to each hour. Further, he said that if you want to increase your income you must bring more value to each hour.

How do you do that? You do it by investing in yourself and becoming more. Rita is a living example of that. I called Rita yesterday and I had not talked to her in about 10 years. I wanted to verify some of the things that I remembered for accuracy in this book. We talked for about an hour.

She shared with me something that really touched my heart and I'll paraphrase for you. She said that she was living in poverty when she came to work for us. Further, she said that she was able to purchase a house and who could have believed that she would ever be able to do that? She moved on and became a successful insurance agent and re-married.

Then she said something that I never even realized. She said, "Roger, after you left me a voice mail this morning, I asked the Lord what I should tell you. I want you to know that I never could have done this without your support and encouragement. When I would make a mistake with pricing or anything else, you would just tell me not to worry. You always told me just to learn the lessons, that it's okay to make mistakes and we grow by doing. So go do. If you would have shamed me I would have quit and stopped the doing."

As Darren Hardy once said, "Remember this: The doer makes mistakes. Mistakes come from doing. But so does success. So go make some mistakes today." You can be all that God intended for you to be. You can reach your human potential, but you must get busy doing and making mistakes. Find a mentor who can encourage you and support you and get busy doing. It would be my pleasure to be that mentor.

God Bless

Service Call Script Templates

Service Agreement Greeting and Presentation

Step 1: Get their agenda

Tech: *Hi Mrs. Jones, I'm _____. Thank you for letting us come out. I'm here to do your system check.*
Ask questions and listen. Some questions that you may ask.
Any frustrations or concerns?
Is there anything you'd like me to look at specifically while I'm here?

Step 2: Express your agenda and get agreement

Tech: *May I give you my service agreement talk so you'll be comfortable with what I'm going to do. Is that okay?*
The reason I'm here is to make sure that your system is reliable, efficient and safe.

Tech: *I don't expect to find anything but If find a concern with something, what I would like to do is bring it to your attention and then you can guide me as to what you would like to do, If anything.*
How does that sound?

Are we okay on time?
Good I'll be there around _____ and if I need you I'll find you.

Presentation Script
While Fulfilling Service Agreement

Tech: *Mrs. Jones, is there a place we can sit down and go over everything that I saw?*

Your system is working fine. However, I do want to bring something to your attention. I do have a concern with _____. You don't have to do anything. However, if you don't, you may have a breakdown. Would you like to be proactive and look at some options or just wait until it breaks?

DO NOT PRESENT OPTIONS WITHOUT AGREEMENT

*The top option takes care of my main concern **plus** other things that could break due to age. You would ONLY want to choose the option if you want your system more reliable and better than it was before I showed up. If you* *choose this option I will* (read description of included services for top option).

This option is $_____. **BUT** *we have all these other options. What would you like to do?*

How to respond to questions about options

Tech: *That's a good question, I hear that a lot.*
The bottom choice is why I am here.
It takes care of the single concern.
As you go up, you gain reliability by fixing other things that commonly break due to age. That's why you get a better warranty.
As you go up even further you gain efficiency. I'm going to make it better than it was before I showed up.
And the top option helps ensure that I won't need to see you again for a long time.

Trouble Call Greeting and Presentation

Tech: *Hi Mrs. Jones, I'm _____. Thanks for having us out. How can I help you today?*

Just to confirm, did the office tell you about the service charge fee of_____?

Let me share with you how I do things so you'll be comfortable. I'll go ahead and get my tools and take a look at the problem. When I determine what's wrong, I would like to sit down with you and go over your options and then you can tell me what to do. How does that sound?

Tech: *Mrs. Jones, do you have a place where we can sit down and go over your options? I do have a concern. I found an issue with _____, but don't worry, I can fix it.*

(If the following applies)
Your system is of the age where some of our clients consider replacing. Do you want to fix it or replace it?

*I am going to show you several options to take care of your problem. The top option takes care of my initial concern **PLUS** other things that could break after I leave due to age. **You would want to pick the top option if you want your system fixed, more reliable and better than it was before I showed up.** If you choose that option I will (read description of included services for top option).*

*If you choose that option it is $_____ **BUT** I do have all these other options. What would you like to do?*

How to respond to questions about options

That's a good question and I hear that a lot. The bottom option is why I am here. As you go up you gain reliability. That's why you get a better warranty. And the top option helps ensure that I won't need to see you again for a long time. What would you like to do?

Water Heater Script

Mrs. Jones, your system is working fine and you are good to go, BUT I did find a **concern** *with your water heater. Your tank is past its average life by x years. When it goes it could leak slow or it could just burst. If it bursts it is a mess and sometimes even an insurance claim.*

A lot of our clients choose to be proactive and move ahead of the event. Would you like to look at some options for a new water heater or just wait until it leaks or burst.

(Embrace the silence)

Let me go out to my truck and get by book and we can sit down and discuss it.

Mrs Jones do you have a place where we can sit down and go over all of your options?

The top option is much more that just a new water heater. You would only want to choose the top option if you want instant hot water at your fixture of choice plus much faster delivery to showers and sinks; the longest warranty possible; protection against possible water damage due to premature tank failure; and more reliability due to restoration of all related components and connections.

If you choose the top option I will (read description of included services for top option). *If you choose this option it is $_____,* ***BUT WE HAVE ALL THESE OTHER OPTIONS. WHAT WOULD YOU LIKE TO DO?***

(Embrace the silence)

How to respond to questions about options

That is a good question and I hear it a lot. The bottom option takes care of main concern. As you go up you get more reliability; added protection against water damage; better warranty; and the top option gives you all of that plus instant hot water. **What would you like to do?**

Made in the USA
Coppell, TX
05 December 2020